Inventing Joy

INVENTING JOY
GEORGE SZIRTES

THE **BLACK SPRING**
PRESS GROUP

First published in 2022
An Eyewear Publishing book, The Black Spring Press Group
Grantully Road, Maida Vale, London w9
United Kingdom

Typeset by User Design, Illustration and Typesetting, UK
Cover art by George Szirtes

ISBN-13 978-1-915406-05-7

TABLE OF CONTENTS

INTRO: INVENTING JOY

Now as the air cools
and evening withdraws into
its own shade, the leaves

hold very still, waiting
for the usual conclusions.
Nothing's concluded

the birds suggest. Sing
something of night. Invent joy
and let it thunder

quietly, like this.

1

THE HARD DAYS

Plucked out of silence,
the faint sound of a pulsing
universe, the breath

a leaf takes at night,
the noise of rain drying, light
dusting off its wings

before vanishing.
There's something under the skin
of the planet: flesh,

blood, bone, the hard days.

REFUGEE

Meeting refugees
is much like meeting yourself
in a dull mirror.

Can you see yourself?
Is that really you? Your eyes
are familiar

but I can't place you.
The matter of place meets time
when it no longer

matters. What's your name?

NOSTALGIE

To have said goodbye
to your birthplace does not mean
it has let you go.

It is waiting there,
lounging outside a station,
the metro perhaps,

kids you once played with
now grown up with a certain
sourness in the mouth,

nodding as you pass.

DISTANCE

Sometimes they return
with familiar faces
made strange by distance.

Whether miles or years
have changed them is hard to tell
yet they are the same.

Sometimes music burns
its way into memory
with its faint singed smell

of woodsmoke and soil.

A MATTER OF TRANSLATION

In this translation
of an old Hungarian
folksong there is a

misunderstanding.
Such misunderstandings are
unfortunately

common. Never mind.
We will have corrected it
several times now

so you understand.

2

I AM ONE

There are too many
things in the world, too many
to hold, hear, and smell.

I'm lost among them,
the way they keep opening
their arms for ever.

I am the sunlight
and the darkness hidden in
the curtain at night.

Next year I will rain.

AUTOBIOGRAPHY

What will you be when
you grow up? Have you grown up?
It was yesterday

or the day before
when you arose, suddenly,
from your father's lap

into adulthood.
Why do you believe in time
or space? Your father

is here. Let him in.

TOBACCO

I meet my father
in a dream. He is standing
at a tall mirror.

He enters it. I
follow. We emerge from it
like a double act.

Leaves are drifting down
an alley. Scent of autumn
and tobacco. Wait,

I call after him.

GHOSTS

Speakers Corner is
silent. The ghosts are leaving.
There are no speeches

to be made today
except by ghosts. That was then,
say the silences.

That was long ago.
I once stood there mesmerised
to hear them harangue

the ghosts they once knew.

THE GIFT

In dreams you are lost
in a bare station forecourt
anxiously waiting

to meet somebody.
Soon it is dusk and you wake
just as the train leaves.

Reader, it is late.
Take out a comb. The mirror
offers you your face

as it might a gift.

3

BEFORE LIGHTS OUT

What are you writing?
*The light in the room before
it goes off.* And then?

*The shadows words leave
on the page.* Can you read them?
What I can read is

the turned-off light. Where
are the words? *They are waiting
to speak in the time*

the bright room leaves them.

GARDEN DREAM

In the dream garden
there are circuitous paths
and a range of trees,

some fallen, most straight
and full of leaves. Where have I
seen such trees before?

How did they appear
as if out of nothing, tall,
overshadowing,

with their dreamless arms?

NOW THAT IT IS LATE

Now that it is late
and night mutters to itself
in quiet corners,

recalling some vague
nightmare that it can't forget
and must keep dreaming,

there remains the moon,
whose gleaming ambivalence
is of little help,

not even in dreams.

NIGHTMARE

Sometimes a nightmare
is the last thing. Other times
it is just a face

rising from a book.
There are cities, hotels, doors,
inconsequential

props thrown together
without consequence. You wake
from yours in a sweat

assembling your life.

WOODLAND SCENE

Somewhere in the wood
are the footprints of those
not yet out of it.

Let's try to find them.
The wood is full of footprints
after all. The trees

grow densely there. Earth
is soft and receptive. Tread
carefully and leave

no prints of your own.

4

CLOCKING OFF

They were at their desks
in the vast office. They pressed
keys and opened files.

They were sinking. Light
swallowed them. When they clocked off
they shrank a little,

each evening shorter
and thinner. You could hear their
faint conversations

like burning paper.

DEMAND

We are entitled
to ask about the plot-line
that is full of holes,

about the motive
driving the lead characters,
about the flowers

in their buttonholes
and the poor cut of their suits.
What do we not know?

What may we demand?

MYANMAR

"They were killing us like chickens"
    Anonymous

They were killing us
like chickens, said the chicken
who was a person

not a chicken. Guns
were being pointed and fired
and they were dying.

The military
were at their dinner. They carved
and praised the chickens

who would keep clucking.

L'AGE D'OR

Having reached l'Age d'Or
they were set fair. This wasn't
Luis Buñuel

or Dalí. This was
Mount Perfection. Down below
the landscape was clear.

The past had to go.
The lumber had to go. Now
they were justified.

Everything must burn.

CLOSE THING

Skin-deep, moment-thin,
you wake from your bed alive
as rain, as fluent

in your medium
as weather when it is brief
and flirtatious, coy

as your future, lost
as your head, your Hamlet wits
not quite at their ends

but shaky, nonplussed.

5

ROMANTIC

Youth likes hints of death
as a psychedelic drug.
I myself liked it.

I liked to feel it
floating to the clear surface
of my poetry

as a dark study
in mortality that would
somehow weight words that

float all too close now.

TRAGEDY

There is tragedy
in the cupboard: you will know
it by its manner.

There are other forms
you might decently adopt
for a rainy day.

Unbearable grief
and dreaded loss are always
seeking their true form,

each with its named blade.

QUEUE

Form an orderly
queue, says Death, then pushes in.
I'll have the hindmost,

he declares. Death takes
what he wants when he wants it.
He has no manners

only sharp elbows.
Listen Death, can't you grow up?
Can't you just let be?

What are queues to you?

MASK

They were wearing masks,
nothing sinister: sequins,
feathers, Venetian,

carnivalesque, trim.
Now where to go? The streetlights
were gathering moths,

the windows were closed
with curtains drawn. It was time
for another place

and the masks felt tight.

GHOST FISH

The aquarium
was empty. Ghosts of fish swam
in diminishing

circles. Fronds trembled
around them. It had been good
while it lasted. Soon

the lights would go off
leaving an unearthly glow.
Mortality stinks,

one ghost fish remarked.

OUTRO: EVEN

Her breath is even,
deep as night. The whole earth breathes
beside her. They sleep

as one, breathing out
together. And beyond night
the dark universe

is rolling in dreams
of enormous vacancy
rolled up in starlight

and small even breaths.